MEMOIRS
OF
JOSEPH BEAUMONT

CAMBRIDGE UNIVERSITY PRESS
Cambridge, New York, Melbourne, Madrid, Cape Town,
Singapore, São Paulo, Delhi, Mexico City

Cambridge University Press
The Edinburgh Building, Cambridge CB2 8RU, UK

Published in the United States of America by Cambridge University Press, New York

www.cambridge.org
Information on this title: www.cambridge.org/9781107623170

First published 1934
Re-issued 2013

A catalogue record for this publication is available from the British Library

ISBN 978-1-107-62317-0 Paperback

MEMOIRS

OF

JOSEPH BEAUMONT

MASTER OF PETERHOUSE 1663–1699
REGIUS PROFESSOR OF DIVINITY IN THE
UNIVERSITY OF CAMBRIDGE 1674

ANNOTATED BY

THOMAS ALFRED WALKER

M.A., LL.D. (CANTAB.)
LITT.D. (VICT. MANCHESTER)
F.S.A., F.R.HIST.S.
SENIOR FELLOW OF PETERHOUSE
SOMETIME RECTOR OF WITNESHAM
SUFFOLK

CAMBRIDGE
AT THE UNIVERSITY PRESS
1934

To

FIELD-MARSHAL SIR WILLIAM RIDDELL BIRDWOOD

Baronet

G. C. B., G. C. S. I., G. C. M. G.

Hon. LL.D. Cambridge, Melbourne and Sydney

Hon. D.C.L. Durham

Master of Peterhouse since 1931

this small book is dedicated.

Son, nephew and brother of Peterhouse men who have served their King and Country in their generation, and more particularly in India, he has added to inherited Collegiate a National Patriotism which has won for him world-wide fame.

The justification for the offering of this brochure is its connection with not the least notable of his predecessors in the Mastership.

FOREWORD

THE MS. transcribed herein, and annotated, fell into my hands years ago as a gleaning from the collection of a London antiquarian bookseller. I recognized its provenance and character, and judged that it was worth permanent preservation. I actually included it amongst items appearing in the List of Books and Manuscripts by or concerning Peterhouse men which I published in 1924 as *A Peterhouse Bibliography*. The MS. was, however, my personal property, albeit I had thought that it might well find a final resting-place in the Library, which had been for a long period entrusted to my special guardianship.

The present publication may serve as a Supplement to *Admissions to Peterhouse* (1615–1911), containing, as it does, particular additional information concerning certain entrants—which I only garnered after 1924 as Rector of Witnesham. The invaluable *Alumni Cantabrigienses*, prepared with special care and amazing persistence by the present President of Queens' and his father, Dr John Venn, has now facilitated the labours of biographers, and placed all Cambridge readers under obligations. The undoubted fact that an occasional error has crept into the classic *Dictionary of National Biography* need not reduce our admiration for the work of Sir Leslie Stephen and his aides-de-camp.

T. A. W.

9 *May* 1934

INTRODUCTION

JOHN GEE, a Cambridge-born youth, educated at the "Public School" at Bishop Stortford, was on 4 July 1719, being then seventeen years of age, admitted Pensioner of Peterhouse under the Tutorship of Godfrey Washington.[1]

On the 29th of the following month he was admitted to a Woodward Scholarship, and two years later was advanced to a more important emolument on the Hale Foundation.

He doubtless owed his promotions to Beaumont influence. A senior John Gee, in whom we may with some confidence identify his father, was Butler and trusty Factotum of Dr Charles Beaumont, whose house across the street became under its owner's will the College Lodge; when the faithful servitor obtained a handsome legacy in the form of certain adjoining properties, which were destined after sundry conveyances, and after some two hundred years, to reach the hands of the Peterhouse Society and to constitute the site of new College buildings.

The younger John graduated in 1723 and proceeded M.A. in 1727. In 1725/6 he was nominated to a Ramsey Fellowship (a *Bye Fellowship*), which was in the alternate presentation of the Master of Peterhouse.

Ordained Deacon at Ely on 19 December 1725, he took Priest's Orders on 17 March 1727/8. Already in 1726 (? 1726/7) he became Vicar of Stapleford,[2] and in 1729 was instituted as Vicar of Burwell. On 29 May 1734 he was (*on the presentation of John Gee*) instituted as Rector and Vicar of Moulton. He obtained the same year a dispensation to continue to hold his old Vicarage (described in *Gent. Magazine*, IV, 276, as that of *Barnwell*) with the Vicarage of Moulton. Those were glorious days for men of easy conscience, and some physical activity; the pluralist was probably a strong rider, and may have employed a resident curate at one or other of the villages.

He was interested in Antiquarianism, and a leading member of an institution founded at Cambridge under the name of the Zodiac Club.[3]

In 1749 he published a collection of the *Original Poems in English and Latin of Dr Joseph Beaumont*, with an Account of his Life and Writings.

---

[1] *Admissions to Peterhouse or S. Peter's College*, p. 241.

[2] Dr Charles Beaumont, the Benefactor, who died on 13 March 1726/7, was Vicar of Stapleford. He bequeathed to his protégé, John Gee, all his books and a handsome estate.

[3] See an Article by Mr R. Bowes in Camb. Antiq. Soc. *Communications*, XIII (1909).

In the MS., which we are now handling, we may unhesitatingly identify materials collected for the above-mentioned "Life of the Author". His informants would be principally members of that Beaumont family, to whom he must have looked up as patrons.

John Gee died on 9 February 1772.

His Will (*P.C.C.*) marks the progress made by the worthy Butler's stock.

William Gee, of County Cambridge, aged seventeen, followed John to the Peterhouse Pensioners' Table on 29 June 1749, and passed the requisite qualifying examination on November 9. On the 18th of the same month he was admitted to a Cosin Scholarship; he had a fresh promotion on 29 April 1751, and graduated in June 1753. Ordained Deacon at Norwich in March 1753, he was not advanced to the priesthood until 18 December 1756, and that at Lincoln. He was Vicar of Wherstead from 1761 to 1815. He became Lecturer of Bentley, Suffolk, in 1770 and in 1772 Rector of S. Stephen's, Ipswich. He held his three benefices in plurality until his death at the age of eighty-four on 19 April 1815. He was buried in the churchyard of S. Stephen's, where a monument records his name and those of his two wives. His second wife, Benjamina, was the widow of the Rev. Peter Hingeston, the pluralist Rector of Capel, and sprang from the Cornwallis family.[1] John Gee's stilted panegyric of Dr Joseph Beaumont, with its overflowing piety and stout Churchmanship, affords, when tested by the pluralism of the writer and his compeers, a curious picture of the conditions of Religious Opinion in the days of Good Queen Anne and the Early Hanoverians.

There were great Preachers in those days, as there were great Generals and great Admirals; but one almost sighs for the atmosphere of Bushido.

---

[1] *Peterhouse Admissions*, p. 294. *Gent. Mag.* XL, 240; LXXXV, 90; XCVI, 503.

MEMOIRS[1] OF JOSEPH BEAUMONT

of Hadleigh and Tattingston etc.

Author of "Psyche" written at Hadleigh.

Some Strictures of ye Life of Dr Joseph Beaumont.

[1] The MS. has been transcribed with the closest possible attention to detail even to some curiosities in the way of spelling and punctuation, although the proceeding was not always exciting. It enshrines the ideas of a Cambridge antiquarian and genealogist of the Age of Thomas Gray.

Some Brief Memoirs relating to Joseph Beaumont, D.D.:

Master of S. Peter's College and Regius Professor in Divinity.

Mr John Beaumont of Hadley[1] had seven children, viz. four sons John, *Joseph*, Edward and William—and three daughters, Sarah, Anna and Mary.

> *Joseph* was born in Hadly March 13, 1615.
>
> > Baptized March 21. His Sponsors were his Uncle Clark[2] and Uncle Parsons, his Aunt Jones and his Aunt Brag.
>
> Sent to Peterhouse in Cambr. 1631.[3]
>
> Chosen Fellow there about 1635.[4]
>
> Made an Oration upon ye 5th of Novembr before ye University 1640.
>
> Ejected from his Fellowship by ye Earl of Manchester 1644.

He received a Letter from R. Quarles[5] dated Jan. 16, 1644, who writes thus—"When a full Dividend is received I will pay your Income, and not only so but if it please God that there be an Agreemt, I shall restore unto You all ye Profits of ye Fellowship as I before desired Ds Glanvil[6] to certify you.

Yours—R. Quarles".

He was presented (by Bp Wren as appears by some letters from that Prelate) to ye Rectory of Kelshall in Hertfordshire 1643.[7]

---

[1] For Pedigree of Beaumont of Hadleigh see *post*. John Beaumont of Hadleigh, a younger son, died 12 May 1653, aet. 69.

[2] ? Edward Clarke of East Bergholt.

[3] Born 13 March 1615/16. Admitted Pensioner 26 April 1631. Slade Scholar June 8. One of the first two Chapel Clerks in the new Peterhouse Chapel 6 March 1632/3. B.A. 1634/5, M.A. 1638, S.T.P. 1660. See *Peterhouse Admissions*, p. 42.

[4] *Fellow of Peterhouse* 1636: ejected 1644.

[5] *Robert Quarles*, 5th son of Francis Quarles of Ufford, Northants. B.A. Trin. 1635, M.A. 1639. Intruded *Fellow of Peterhouse* 1644. *Bursar* 1644–6.

[6] *Joseph Glanvil* (admitted as Glanfield). Of Co. Suffolk: like Beaumont, seemingly, a native of Hadleigh. B.A. Pet. 1641, M.A. 1646. Perne Scholar and Librarian 1641. Rector of Wimbish 1660: succeeded on death in 1680 by *Maurice Glanville*. See a later note as to an identification in *D.N.B.*

[7] Bishop Wren persisted in the exercise of his episcopal functions whilst in prison in the Tower, where he remained until the Restoration. The early collations of Joseph Beaumont to various benefices were amongst these typical acts of defiance. The date of that to Kelshall was probably 1643/4.

He was Chaplain to yᵉ said Bishop & Tutour to his sons,[1] whom in those Tumultous Times he instructed at Hadly his Native Place, where at his leisure hours he composed his Psyche.

He was presented By Bp Wren to Elm with yᵉ chappel of Emneth[2] vacated by ye Death of Robert Dove—1646.

To yᵉ seventh canon and Prebend of Ely vacated by ye Death of John Buckerridg Feb. 18 1647.[3]

He married the Bishop's Daughter in Law, Elizabeth Brownrigg Daughter of Merchant Brownrigg of Ipswich (born in ye House of her Grandfathʳ Mr Cutler at yᵉ Chauntry in Sproughton[4] and baptized there).

The Rites were solemnized by his Friend Mr John Tolly,[5] who was also an

[1] (a) *Matthew Wren* (eldest son of the Bishop). Born in Peterhouse 20 Aug. 1621, where his father was Master. Admitted Fellow Commoner of Peterhouse (*aet.* 14) 25 Oct. 1642, *sub tutelâ et fide-jussione Mri Beaumont*, having been *educatus paternis in aedibus*. M.A. Oxon. 1661, F.R.S. 1663. Was with Charles II at the Battle of Worcester. After the Restoration, M.P. for S. Michael's, Secretary to Clarendon and to James, Duke of York. Died in 1672, whilst in the Duke's service. Last Will made on board "the *Royal Prince*". Buried in Pembroke Chapel, Cambridge. *Author*. See *Peterhouse Admissions*, p. 74. The second son of the Bishop was

(b) *Thomas Wren*. Baptised at Little S. Mary's 20 Jan. 1632/3. M.D. Oxon. 2 Aug. 1660 (by Chancellor's Letter). F.R.S. Archdeacon of Ely 1663 (then described as LL.D.). Sinecure Rector of Littlebury 1660 until death. Rector of North Wold 1661–2; of Willingham 1662–79. Canon of Ely 1662–79; of Southwell 1664–79. Prebendary of Willenhall in Wolverhampton 1660–79. Died in October 1679; buried at Wilburton Oct. 24. He obviously owed most of his appointments to his father. See *Peterhouse Admissions*, p. 120. For pedigree of Wren see *Genealogist*, N.S. 1, 262.

[2] Rector of Elm and Emneth, Cambs 1645.

[3] Dr Venn makes it 1651. The favoured priest was effectively instituted as Prebendary in September 1660.

[4] Now the property of the Ipswich Corporation by benefaction of Sir Arthur Churchman.

Benjamin Cutler, of Co. Suffolk, was admitted Pensioner of Peterhouse 28 June 1631. Perne Scholar 6 Sept. 1631. *Fellow Commoner* 1632. He was created M.A. Oxon. 31 Aug. 1636. (*Al. Oxon.*) He became seated at the Chantry and a J.P. As "son and heir of *Thomas* Cutler of Ipswich, Suffolk, Esq.", he was admitted at Gray's Inn 15 March 1638/9. He was fined for being in Arms against the Parliament; *East Anglian*, pp. 1–166.

Thomas Cutler, *armiger*, gave £20 to John Cosin's Chapel Fund. In 1632–3 he gave a large silver bowl beautifully gilt, and engraved with his own and the College Arms, for use in the receipt of alms at Solemn Eucharist in Peterhouse Chapel. *Computus Roll*, 1632–3.

Robert Cutler of the Chantry had a Grant of Arms in 1612. He was Portman of Ipswich.

For Pedigree see *Visit. of Suffolk* 1664/8, p. 136. "Daughter in Law", of course, = Step-daughter.

[5] *John Tolly*. B.A. Christ's 1632/3, M.A. Pet. 1636.

Admitted Pensioner of Christ's 8 April 1629: son of John Tolly: born in London: School, under Mr Farnaby: age 15. Admitted 4 Jan. 1633/4, at Peterhouse, being then B.A. of Christ's. Perne Scholar 6 March. Perne Fellow 1633–4. *Fellow* 1635.

ejected Fellow of Peterhouse, in Putney Church May 7, 1650. He settled
at his Wife's Estate at Tattisdon [Tattingston] near Ipswich, where he had
by her four sons, Joseph, John, William and Charles, and Two Daughters,
Elizabeth and Anna Susanne.

Joseph his second child was born Jan. 8, 1652, and baptized by Dr
Ball Jan. 13.[1] Mr Beaumont of Hadley his Grandfather, Mr Joseph
Clark and Mrs Keen were his Sponsors.

Died May 16, 1654.

Elizabeth, his first child, was born Feb. 7, 1651.

Baptized May 11 by Dr Ball according to ye rites of ye Church of Engl.
Her Godfathers were Ben Cutler,[2] Dr Matt. Wren, Her Godmothers
Anna and Susanna Wren.

Died March 5 ye same year, and buried according to ye Form in our
Liturgy in Tatingston Church.

John[3] born July 18, 1654, baptized by Edm^d Duncon Curate.

His Godf. Edward Beaumont,[4] John Clark.[5]

His Godm. Mrs Keen, Mrs Beaumont the Grandmother.

Anna Susanna born and baptized July 1656 by Edmd Duncon. Godf.
Ben Cutler, Matt. Wren. Godmothers Anna Wren and Susanna Wren.

Bursar 1638–9. Took his M.A. from Peterhouse in 1636. Was ejected from his
Fellowship in 1644. Rector of Tattingston 1641. Rector of Little Gransden, ejected
thence in 1645. Will (P.C.C.) 1655. Peile, I, 399. *Peterhouse Admissions*, p. 50.

[1] This is repeated in the MS. after the record concerning the child Elizabeth.
"Mr Beaumont" is John Beaumont (ob. 1653). "Mr Joseph Clark" may be Joseph
Clarke of Washbroke, clerk, son of Edward Clarke of East Bergholt. His son was
Edward Clarke of Bentley, gent. in 1664. *Visit.* 1664–8, p. 112.

[2] Benjamin Cutler, of the Chantry, J.P. Perne Scholar of Peterhouse 1631.

[3] John Beaumont. Admitted Pensioner (aged 17) of Peterhouse 27 June 1671.
M.A. (*Lit. Reg.*) 1675. Ordained Deacon and Priest at Norwich 1680. Rector of
Tattingston 1680. Became Lord of the Manor of Tattingston and Patron of the
Benefice under the Will of his father.

[4] Edward Beaumont, younger brother of Joseph, and so uncle of the child.

[5] John Clarke, 'of East Bergholt, gent.', in 1664, son of Edward by Martha
Woodgate. He married Rose, daughter of Richard Glanville of Hadleigh. (*Visit.*
1664–8, p. 132.) The Glanvilles (otherwise Glanfields) were a Hadleigh family, which
sent up many recruits to Peterhouse (see *Peterhouse Admissions*, pp. 65, 67, 119, 144,
150), including a younger Richard, who came up in 1671 under the Tutorship of John
Glanville, *Fellow* (ob. 1683). Even the *D.N.B.* has gone astray on Joseph Glanvil
(Glanfield), M.A. Pet. 1646, sometime Perne Scholar, and confused him with a more
famous Joseph Glanvil (ob. 1680), Rector of S. Peter and S. Paul, Bath, F.R.S., and
a distinguished author. The Bath Rector was a Devonian. The Peterhouse namesake,
M.A. 1646, was Rector of Wimbish, where he died, unfortunately in the same year as
the greater Divine; and was succeeded by yet another Peterhouse Suffolk-born man,
Maurice Glanvil (see *Peterhouse Admissions*, p. 150). I was myself at one time misled
by the similar names. T. A. W.

She died of ye Small Pox at Peterhouse April 14, 1674, and was buried in ye chancel of Little St Maries.[1] Aged 17.

William[2] born Dec. 5, 1658, baptized Dec. 11 by his Fath^r. His sureties were Joseph Beaumont of Hadley and the wife of Edward Beaumont.

Charles[3] born Oct. 11, 1660, baptized by his Father in Tatingston Church. That very Day the Public Service was restored.

His sureties were Thomas, Charles and Mary Wren.

In ye Year 1653 He received a Letter from ye B^p of Kilmore[4] wherein ye Bishop begs his Charity complaining that he had fourteen daily to provide for, and not sixpence to go to Market with.

He received also another Letter wherein ye Bishop makes a very thankful acknowledgment of his Great Liberality.

He took Legal and full Posses^n of ye Prefermt^s to which he had been some years before presented—namely Kelshall—The Canonry—and Elm (into which last one Jackson had intruded) Anno 1660.

By a Mandamus from ye King he with Mapletoft and Holbeach received the Degree of D^r, and became Chaplain to his Majesty, and was instituted,

---

[1] Anna Beaumont, daughter of Dr Joseph Beaumont, was buried at Little S. Mary's, 15 April 1674. *Little St Mary's Reg.*

[2] William Beaumont. Admitted Pensioner (aged 17) of Peterhouse 10 Jan. 1675. B.A. 1678/9, M.A. 1682. Perne Fellow 1680. Died 1686. Buried at Little S. Mary's, Cambridge, Oct. 3, 1686. *Peterhouse Admissions*, p. 154; Venn, *Alumni*.

[3] Charles Beaumont. Admitted Pensioner (aged 15) of Peterhouse 10 June 1675. B.A. 1678/9, M.A. 1682, S.T.P. 1720. Ramsey Fellow 1680. Died 17 March 1726/7, in his house opposite the College, subsequently the Lodge. Buried in the College Chapel next his father. Vicar of Stapleford 1686. Edited his father's "Psyche" 1702. Residuary Legatee of his father 1699. *Benefactor* of Peterhouse, to which he bequeathed his house and £1555 to be invested in Advowsons. A Portrait in the Lodge and another (a panel) in the College Hall. The College purchased the Advowsons of four Suffolk benefices, Freckenham, Norton, Newton by Sudbury and Witnesham, the last being a family living recently acquired by a branch of the Beaumonts (Beaumonts of Ipswich). *Peterhouse Admissions*, p. 154; Venn, *Alumni*.

Dr Charles Beaumont bequeathed property to his "faithful servant" John Gee (his Butler and Factotum) including a house adjoining his own, opposite the College. John Gee, seemingly the faithful servant's son and doubtless the protégé of the Doctor, whom he succeeded as Vicar of Stapleford, became Ramsey Fellow in 1725/6. He was the writer of the *Memoirs of the late Joseph Beaumont*, whose *Miscellaneous Poems* he published in 1749, prefixing a Life of the poet, although in so doing he offended in kindly fashion against the express instructions of "Magnus Josephus".

[4] The Bishop of Kilmore in 1653 was Robert Maxwell, who succeeded the great scholar William Bedell in the fatal year 1643. Of him I know nothing. The predecessor of Bedell as Bishop of Kilmore was Thomas Moigne (1613–29), S.T.B. Pet. 1594 (ob. 1 Jan. 1628/9), *Fellow of Peterhouse* 1587 and sometime Bursar, for whom see *Peterhouse Biog. Reg.* II, 64. He was savagely attacked by Bishop Bedell's chaplain, son-in-law and biographer.

and by Proxy inducted, into ye Rectory of Gransden Parva[1] in ye same year viz. 1660.

Into this Living one Jessop had intruded, and continued in Possess^n of it some time after ye Restorat^n. Among some Orders from Dr Matt. Wren, B^p of Ely, concerning a Visitat^n to be held in Cambridge, the Commissioners are required to call Dr Lucas as ye Right Incumbent of Little Gransden, and that Jessop who had been denied a License to preach there anno 1662 should be examined by what Authority he officiates there and whether he pretends to have a License from ye See of Canterbury.

He preached at Suffolk Feast in Bow Church Lond^n 1660. For which he was presented with a Silver Tankard inscribed

Suffolcie Tibi Nobis.

Dr Joseph Beaumont was Minister of Trinity Parish in Ely 1661.

Dr Beaumont's wife died at his House in Ely May 29,[2] 1662, and was buried in ye Cathedral behind ye Altar, aged 38 years and five months.

He was by B^p Wren made Master of Jesus College, Cambr., vacated by y^e cess^n of John Pearson D.D. April 17, 1662.

He had y^e Living of Conington 1663, and [was] chosen into y^e Mastership of Peterhouse y^e same year, vacated by y^e Death of Bernard Hale D.D.

He was instituted into y^e Rectory of Teversham anno 166$\frac{3}{4}$

And into y^e Rectory of Barley in Hertfordshire June 22, 1664.

Dr Boldero Master of Jesus under his Hand and y^e Seal of y^e College acknowledges that he had received of Dr Beaumont The Summ of Ten Pounds as a Free Gift for making y^e Organs & repairing y^e Chappel of y^e same College Octob. 29, 1664.

He was made Regius Profess^r in Divinity anno 1670—by a Mandamus.[3]

Anno 1686 He received a Letter from Joseph Idzi-Kowski, a Polander by Birth and formerly a Priest of ye Roman Church according to ye Order of St Dominic.

He was then residing at Cambridge in which Place he says he had performed some learned Works, and that yet he was destitute of all Things and

---

[1] The Rectory from which John Tolly (*Fellow* of Peterhouse) was ejected by Parliament in 1645.

[2] The *Life* (by J. Gee) makes it May 31. Mrs Beaumont died of consumption before she could be removed to Cambridge.

[3] The date of his appointment to the Regius Professorship (to which was attached the Rectory of Somersham, Hunts) is given by *Alumni Cantabrigienses* and the *University Calendar* as 1674. Peter Gunning, his predecessor as Regius Professor, became Bishop of Chichester in 1670, and was translated to Ely in 1675. The date of the Mandamus would be decisive. J. Gee most clearly writes *1670*.

forsaken of all men. He begged for some Money to carry him to Lyn and from thence into his own Country.

Bryan Walton July 5 1688 sent Dr Beaumont twenty five Pounds for yᵉ use of yᵉ College Chappel.

He made a Funeral oration at yᵉ death of Dr Spenser.

Dr Joseph Beaumont was appointed a Member of yᵉ Ecclesiastical Commission opened in yᵉ Jerusalem Chamber Octob. 10, 1689, but I believe he never appeared there.

He preached at Great St Maries Nov. 5, 1699, and contracting a Fever that Day died on yᵉ 23 of yᵉ same month.

To yᵉ Chappel of Peterhouse he bequeathed[1] £300,

To yᵉ Poor of Little St Maries £20.

He published nothing yᵗ I know of besides

The Poem before mentioned viz. Psyche—and a Little Tract agˢᵗ Dr More.

His valuable Latin MSS. were bequeathed by his son Dr Charles Beaumont to yᵉ Library of Peterhouse.

It may be wondered yᵗ in these Memoirs there is no mention of Time when or Person by whom This Great Man was ordained Deacon and Priest. The Instruments of his Orders I saw after his son's Death, but by some means or other They are since lost. I remember neither yᵉ Dates nor yᵉ Names therein contained but by a letter writ to Him while at Tatingston by Bishop Wren, it appears yᵗ he was ordained by some Prelate to whom he afterwards had an opportunity of extending his Charity. And this might be Dr Brownrig Bᵖ of Exeter and Master of Catharine Hall and a Relation of his wife's—or rather the Poor Bishop of Kilmore mentioned under yᵉ year 1653.

It could hardly be yᵉ former because as I take it our Joseph was in full orders before the Year 1642 till which Time Dr Brownrig was not nominated to ye See of Exeter.

Dr Ball seems to have been Rector of Tatingston[2] and Mr Edmᵈ Duncon his Curate and perhaps his Successor.

Dr Ball married, if I mistake not, one of Bishop Wren's Daughters.

---

[1] Will proved (*V.C.C.*) 1699.

[2] We may identify Dr Ball for John Gee. Richard Ball, Matriculated as Pensioner of Pembroke Michs. 1623, *aet.* 14, son of Richard Ball, of London, Mercer. B.A. 1626/7, M.A. 1630, S.T.B. 1637, S.T.P. (*Lit. Reg.*) 1660. Fellow of Pembroke 1630. Rector of Wilby and of Westerfield 1638–43; of Tattingston 1643; of S. Mary Woolchurch, London 1660–1. Prebendary of Ely 1660; of Lincoln 1660. Rector of Bluntisham, Hunts 1662–84. Master of the Temple 1661–84. Died 6 April 1684. Buried in the Temple Church. Benefactor to Pembroke. See Venn, *Alumni*.

One Richd Ball of Lond^n was admitted at Pembroke Hall, became Fellow 1630, Master of the Temple, Rector of Bluntisham, Prebend of Ely— But the Ball here meant, if I remember, was *John* Ball perhaps ye Son of Richard afore mention.

The reason why the word Priest and Bishop was inserted into the Form of Ordinat^n is Thus given in Dr Burnet's History of the Reformat^n, p. 2, p. 144.

The Reformers in King Edward's Time agreed on a Form of ordaining B^ps Priests and Deacons which is ye same we yet use, except in some words that have been added since (viz. at ye Restorat^n) in ye ordinat^n of a Priest or a B^p. For there was before That no express mention made in ye words of ordaining th^m y^t it was for ye one or the other office, in Both it was said Receive Thou ye H Gh. in ye Name of the Father etc. but that having been since made use (viz. by ye Presbyterians) to prove Both Functions the same, it was altered of late years to what it is now—Nor were These words being ye same in giving Both orders any Ground to infer y^t ye Church esteemed one Order, The rest of ye office shewing ye contrary very plainly.

Doctor having published This within twenty years after ye Thing was done when so many were alive y^t were members of Convocat^n w^n ye Alterat^n was made, and especially Dr Gunning and Dr Pierson who were the prime advisers of it, it is impossible he c^d want True Informat^n in this particular or be so impudent as to impose it upon the world if otherwise y^n he relates, when there were so many in Being who from their own knowledge could convince him of falsity herein.—Dr Prideaux *Validity of ye Orders of ye Church of England* p. 72.

Dr Basire in The Account which he has published of ye Life of This B^p[1] p. 84 tells us that he was brought before a Sacrilegious and Rebellious Assembly of Laymen called ye Grand Committee for Religion—and that there he behaved with such constancy and courage in maintaining The Principles and Rites of ye Church of England that he came off clear from all calumnies laid to his Charge in both Articles and Pamphlets, to the notorious amazem^t disappointm^t and shame of his false Accusers. By way of Appendix to this Page—

[1] The Bishop in question was John Cosin, Bishop of Durham (1660–72), Master of Peterhouse 1635–44 (restored 1660), in succession to Dr Matthew Wren. As Prebendary of Durham, he was vehemently assailed by the wild Puritans Peter Smart and Prynne. When installed in 1640 as Dean of Peterborough, he was, on charges preferred against him by Peter Smart, ordered by the House of Commons into the custody of the Sergeant-at-Arms, and in the following March formally impeached. The story of his interview with the Grand Committee is quoted in *Peterhouse* (College Histories), p. 107.

Mr William Sutton March 25, 1703, writes This Note—

As an Example of his Xⁿ Magnanimity and Patience of mind under his Troubles take what follows communicated to me by an Eminent Divine of yᵉ Church of England now living who in his younger years had ye happiness of being brought up undʳ yᵉ Feet of This Great Gamaliel. When by the Prosecutⁿ of Mr Peter Smart he was brought to appear before yᵉ Grand Committee, and to answer for himself concerning his Use of Certain Ceremonies such as signing with yᵉ Cross, doing Reverence at yᵉ name of Jesus and bowing toward the Altar, at his coming into the Room He made his Obeisance at which one of yᵉ Committee to give him a foretaste of yᵉ kind usage he was to expect at Their Hands crys out—

Doctor Here is no Altar—to which yᵉ Good man makes answer with a Becoming modesty. Then, Sir, I hope there will be no Sacrifice.

ADDENDA

I owe the pedigrees of Beaumont to J. J. Muskett's laborious and generally excellent *Suffolk Manorial Families* (Vol. II).

His Beaumont Pedigrees naturally need an occasional correction. Thus he ascribes to Charles Beaumont, D.D., Fellow and Benefactor of Peterhouse, the Rectory of Witnesham, in the chancel of the church of which village many Beaumonts lie interred, including another Charles Beaumont (ob. 1756) who *was* Rector. Charles Beaumont of Witnesham was a member of the family of *Beaumont of Ipswich*, an offshoot of *Beaumont of Bildeston*, and thus kin of *Beaumont of Hadleigh*.

See also the *Suffolk Visitation*, 1664–8, pp. 156, 165.

The Suffolk Beaumonts claimed a Leicestershire extraction ("out of Leicest^r"). The visiting Herald admitted for them as ARMS: *Azure, a lion rampant within an orb of eight fleurs-de-lis Or* [? *semée of fleurs-de-lis*], *a mullet on the shoulder for difference.* CREST: *A lion passant* [*Or*], *a mullet on the shoulder for difference.*

William Beaumont, grandson of Julian Beaumont of Hadleigh, made the mullet on the shoulder of the lion a mullet on *a crescent for difference.*

Beaumont of Beaumont Hall in Harkstead, Co. Suffolk, undoubtedly descending from Henry, Lord Beaumont, who "came into England with Isabel of France and was her nere cosen", gave at the Suffolk Visitation in 1561 ARMS: *Quarterly 1 and 4, Azure a lion rampant within an orb of eight fleurs-de-lis Or* (Beaumont). *2 and 3, Azure a fess between two chevrons Argent*, impaling Browne quartering Vere. CREST: *A lion passant Or.*[1]

The great Leicestershire house of Beaumont (Beaumont of Cole-Orton) bore in 1619:

ARMS: *Quarterly: 1. Azure, semée of fleurs-de-lis, a lion rampant Or. 2. Azure, three garbs Or, banded Gules. 3. Gules, seven mascles conjoined Or, three, three and one. 4. Gules, a cinque foil ermine pierced. 5. Azure, a lion rampant argent, crowned Or. 6. Argent, an inescocheon within a double tressure flory counterflory Gules. 7. Azure, three garbs Or. 8. Gules, a lion rampant vair. 9. Azure, a fess argent between three cinque foils Or. 10. Argent, a maunch sable, in chief a crescent of the last for difference. 11. Argent, a fess sable between three birds (untinctured). On an escocheon of pretence, three rere-mice displayed gules.* CREST: *On a cap of maintenance azure, semée of fleurs-de-lis Or turned up ermine, a lion rampant of the second.*[2]

---

[1] *Visit. of Suffolk*, 1561, p. 5.   [2] *Visit. of Leicester*, 1619, p. 169.

The stock placed at the head of its pedigree Louis, son of Charles, King of Sicily, who was son of Louis VIII, King of France, he having married Alice, daughter and heiress of "Viscount" Beaumont.[1] Queen Isabella, as a French princess, might well admit "cousinship". The alliances of the house were amongst the noblest in the land. It produced mighty Churchmen, distinguished soldiers, great Judges and, yet more notably, the dramatist, Francis Beaumont.[2] The excellent Suffolk clothiers might be forgiven if they on occasion boasted kinship with Leicestershire. The relation would appeal strongly to Matthew Wren, and none the less in that the alliances included the name of the great favourite Villiers, Duke of Buckingham.

The Beaumonts of Whitley, Co. Yorks, gave in 1612 as ARMS: *Gules, a lion rampant within an orb of 9 crescents argent, charged on the breast with a mullet for difference.* CREST: *A bull's head quarterly, argent and gules, horned, per fesse Or and of the first.*[3]

---

[1] But was he *Viscount*? The first Viscount was John Beaumont, so created in 1440. He was 6th *Baron* Beaumont, and in 1434 was created Count of Boulogne in France. He visited Cambridge in 1445–6, stayed for a night in Pembroke and made an oblation in the College Chapel, which offering appears amongst Parochial Oblations in Peterhouse Accounts (Pembroke Chapel lying within the parochial limits of Little S. Mary's Church). He became K.G. and Constable of the Realm; and, as became his house, fell in the Battle of Northampton in 1459; a loyal Lancastrian. See *Peterhouse Biog. Reg.* I, 45. The Cole-Orton strain were strongly represented on the Peterhouse Boards in Tudor and Early Stuart days. *Sir Thomas Beaumont* of Cole-Orton, who was created Viscount Beaumont of Swords in Ireland, seemingly as some solatium for the higher title patriotically lost by his ancestor, was *Fellow Commoner of Peterhouse* in 1596. *Ibid.* p. 46.

[2] For several of the Leicestershire family, including two of the baptismal name of Francis, see *Peterhouse Biog. Reg.* I, 235, 246, 247.

[3] *Visit. of Yorkshire*, 1612, p. 492. Cf. Dugdale's *Visit. of Yorkshire*, ed. Clay, III, 219.

Adam Beaumont, admitted Fellow Commoner of Sidney (*aet.* 15) in February 1646/7, was son of Thomas Beaumont (afterwards knighted) of Whitley.

The Arms of Beaumont of Whitley, which appear over the Trinity Great Gate, have been pointed out as indicating that *Robert Beaumont*, Master of Trinity, 1561–7, was of the Whitley Beaumont stock, but Messrs Cooper (*Athenae Cantabrigienses*, I, 245) decline to admit it, and rank him as of County Leicester, a ranking which is justified by the *Register of Westminster School*. He was B.A. Trin. 1543/4, M.A. Pet. 1550, B.D. 1560, D.D. 1564. He became *Fellow of Peterhouse* in 1550 (successor 1562/3), *Bursar* 1550–2, Lady Margaret Professor of Divinity 1559–61, Archdeacon of Huntingdon 1560, Canon of Ely 1564. He was Vice-Chancellor 1564–5 and 1566–7, dying in June 1567. Oddly enough, I find no one of his Christian name in the contemporary Cole-Orton pedigree, whilst a namesake does appear as the offspring of a second match in the Whitley Beaumont pedigree. The Westminster School Register holds the field. John Beaumont, Fellow of Trinity 1875, a notable Divine, was also sometime a Westminster Scholar. See *Trinity College Admissions*, II, 45, 78; *Peterhouse Biog. Reg.* I, 136; Dugdale's *Visit. of Yorkshire*, III, 219, 220.

The Beaumonts of Fangfoss, a junior branch, making their Orb of seven crescents, had in 1612 as their senior member "Hamond" Beaumont, whose name repeats itself on the Peterhouse Boards in 1659 and 1700. In the former year the entrant, a Sizar, educated at Pocklington, was *Eboracensis*, and after taking his M.A. became Rector of Elwick, Co. Durham (ob. 1701).[1] The younger "Hammond", admitted as Pensioner on promotion from a Sizarship, and advanced the same year to a Hale Scholarship, was of Co. Durham, educated at Durham School.[2] He took his M.A. in 1707. It is not difficult to guess the ancestry of the pair.

A quick succession of Yorkshire, Durham and Northumbrian youths came up to Peterhouse about the same time under the Tutorship of a favourite Durham-born Fellow, Alexander Bickerton, who had been himself educated at Newcastle School.[3]

The Beaumonts of Whitley claimed descent from Henry, Lord Beaumont, "who came out of Fraunce with Queen Isabell, into England, Edward the II wyff", by his wife, Ales, daughter and heiress of Alexander, Earl of Buchan and Constable of Scotland, a kinsman of the famous Black Comyn, who was slain by the Bruce, whose companions thought it well to "mak syker". The Comyn descended from Hugh Lupus, Earl of Chester, who married a sister of William the Conqueror, and had a son-in-law who was "Erl Bemont and Myllent".[4]

It is clear that the Whitley Beaumonts and those of Beaumont Hall in Harkstead, Co. Suffolk, sprang from a common stock.

---

[1] *Peterhouse Admissions*, p. 118.   [2] *Ibid.* p. 204.
[3] *Ibid.* p. 145.   [4] *Visit. of Yorkshire*, 1564, p. 18.

PEDIGREES

BEAUMONT OF BILDESTON AND COGGESHALL

See MUSKETT, II, 331, 334

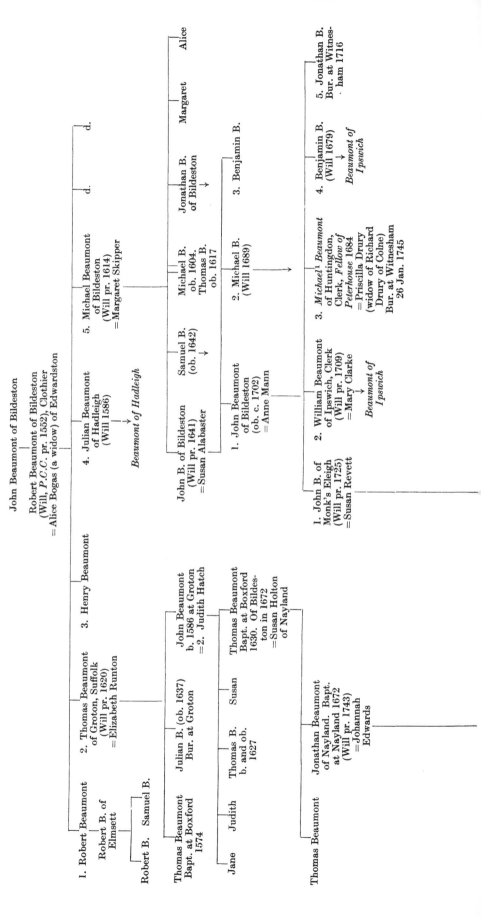

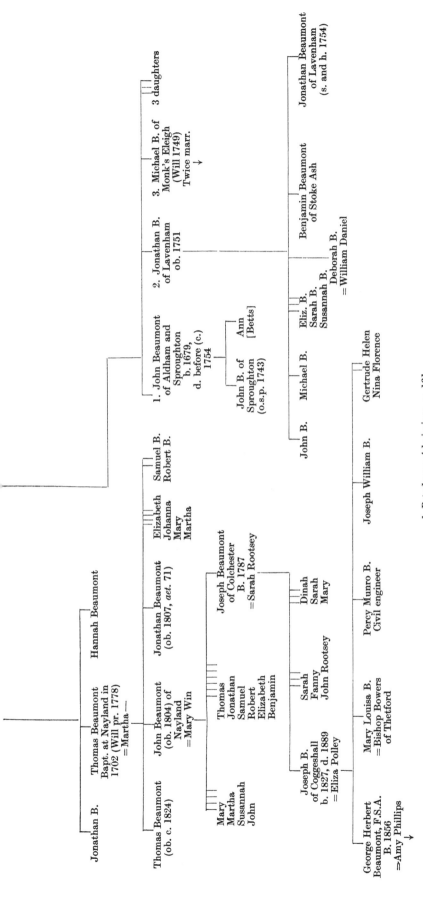

¹ *Peterhouse Admissions*, p. 161.

BEAUMONT OF HADLEIGH

See MUSKETT, II, 333

Robert Beaumont of Bildeston
(s. and h. of John of Bildeston; 1543)
Will made 21 July 1551; pr. 1552
= Alice Bogas (a widow) of Edwardston

1. Robert B.

2. Thomas B. of Groton
Will 1618, pr. 1620
↓
Beaumont of Coggeshall

3. Henry B.

4. Julian B. of Hadleigh
[Will, *P.C.C.* 20 Dec. 1586]
= Sarah, daughter of Edward Gaell
of Hadleigh

5. Michael B. of Bildeston
[Will, *P.C.C.* 1613,
proved 7 Jan. 1614]
M.I. at Bildeston
= Margaret Skipper
↓
Beaumont of Bildeston

Margaret Beaumont

A daughter

1. Edward Beaumont of Hadleigh
Bapt. 1580. Will, *P.C.C.* 23 April,
pr. 10 June 1645
= Alice, d. of Robert Lufkin
of Playford

Sarah B.

Anna B.

2. John Beaumont of Hadleigh
Bapt. 1584. Will, *P.C.C.* 1652,
pr. 1653. M.I. at Hadleigh
= Sarah, daughter of Edward Clarke,
sister and devisee of Edward Clarke
of East Bergholt, High Sheriff
of Suffolk
(Will, *P.C.C.* 1646)

Hannah B. = Samuel Smith
John Smith

Sarah B. = John White of Edwardston [1652]

4. Edward B. b. 1625, d. 1674

3. John B.

2. Blewett B.

1. William B. (s. and h. aet. 9, 1664)

3. William B. d. 1712 =(1) Mary, d. of John Alabaster, (2) Mary, d. of John Blewett of Hadleigh

(3) Ann, d. of William Brunskill

2. Joseph Beaumont b. 13 March 1615. d. 23 Nov. 1699. B.A. 1634/5. M.A. 1638. D.D. 1660. Fellow 1636. Master of Peterhouse 1663–99. Regius Professor of Divinity 1670–99 =Elizabeth, d. and h. of Robert Brownrigg (by Elizabeth Cutler, who married secondly Bishop Matthew Wren), Lady of the Manor of Tattingston

1. John B. b. 1614, d. 1617

Philip B., b. 1615 =Sarah—
Sarah Beaumont [1645]

Joseph B. of Hadleigh, b. 1612 (Will, P.C.C. 1681) =Martha, d. of John Brand of Edwardston

John B. 1608–45

Edward B. b. 1606. Will 1639 =Joan—

3. Charles Beaumont b. 1660. (Will 1725, pr. 1726, 22 Mar.) Ramsey Fellow of Peterhouse and Benefactor. Ob. 1726/7

2. William B. b. 1658. o.s.p. (1686). M.A. 1682. Perne Fellow 1680

1. John Beaumont b. 1654. Lord of Tattingston. M.A. per Lit. Reg. 1675. Parke Fellow 1677. R. of Tattingston 1680

Edward B. (s. and h. 1681). Holds Cockfield Hall and lands in Elmsett
Edward Beaumont (s. and h. 1681)

Joseph B. [s. and h. 1664, aet. 19] o.s.p.

Alice = Thomas Sewell of Great Henney, gent. (1687)

Martha = William Plampin 1631

s.
s.
s.

Mary B. = Thomas Whiting of Hadleigh, gent. (Will 1682)

Penelope B. [Under 17 in 1699]

Anna Susanna B. (=Taster) Devisee under Will of Dr Charles Beaumont in 1725

Caroline B. [Under 17 in 1699]

Mary B. =Joseph Capron of Chigwell, Essex. Legatee in 1699

Elizabeth B. Legatee of another farm in Kettlebaston and Hitcham (1699)

Captain John Beaumont Received farm in Kettlebaston and Hitcham under grandfather's Will (1699)

Joseph Beaumont Received Alston Hall, Stutton, under grandfather's Will (1699)

BEAUMONT OF IPSWICH

See MUSKETT, II, 332

John Beaumont of Bildeston = Anne, d. and h. of William Mann, of Hitcham, gent. (Will 1702)

Anna B. (Bapt. 1645. Will pr. 1705/6) = John Meadows of Bury, Clerk (she being his 3rd wife)

1. John Beaumont of Monk's Eleigh Bapt. 1647. Will pr. 1725 = (1) Susan Revett (2) Ann Danford (widow) →

2. William Beaumont of Ipswich, Clerk. Bapt. 1649. Will pr. 1709. B.A. Cath. 1670/1. M.A. 1674. Rector of Witnesham 1705–8. Rector of Hintlesham 1672 = Mary Clarke

3. *Michael B.*[1] of Huntingdon, Clerk. B.A. Pet. 1681. M.A. 1685. *Fellow of Peterhouse* 1684–93. Rector of Waltham, Lincs. Died suddenly 11 October 1710. Bur. at Witnesham (*Register* there and M.I. in Chancel)

4. Benjamin B. of Ipswich Bapt. 1651. Will 1679 = Elizabeth, daughter of George Southwood

Benjamin B. of Grundisburgh, gent. Will pr. 1733. M.I. at Grundisburgh

5. Jonathan B. (ob. 1716) died suddenly in Barham Church. Buried in the Chancel 26 Dec. 1716 at Witnesham (*Witnesham Reg.*)

Susan B. = William Blomfield

Mary
Sarah (Hammond, later Sparrow)
Abigail
Elizabeth
Deborah [Lufkin]

1. John Beaumont of Ipswich Will 1747. Ob. *aet.* 69 = Sarah Bantoft

Mary B.

Sarah B. = Thomas Lodge

2. Robert Beaumont B.A. Queens' 1704/5. By purchase Patron of Witnesham. M.A. 1708. Bapt. Hintlesham 1683. Will 1737. Rector of Witnesham 1708–27. Vicar of Henley, Suffolk, 1727. Vicar of St Laurence, Ipswich = Priscilla, daughter of Richard Drury of Colne (buried 6 Feb. 1745/6) and stepdaughter of *Michael B.* of Huntingdon, Clerk

3. Michael B. Bapt. 1687. Ob. 1733, *aet.* 46 = Elizabeth Burrough

John B. ob. 1717

Michael B. ob. 1719

4. Thomas B. Bapt. 1691. Dead in 1709

5. William B.

William B. ob. 1732, *aet.* 7

Mary B.
Sarah B.

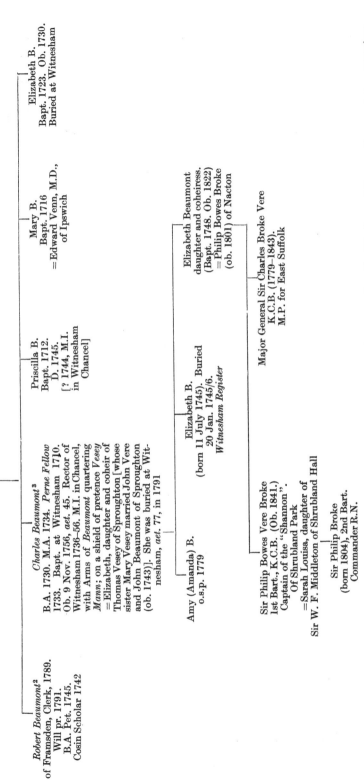

Robert Beaumont[2]
of Framsden, Clerk, 1789.
Will pr. 1791.
B.A. Pet. 1745.
Cosin Scholar 1742

Charles Beaumont[3]
B.A. 1730. M.A. 1734. Perne Fellow
1733. Bapt. at Witnesham 1710.
Ob. 9 Nov. 1756, aet. 45. Rector of
Witnesham 1736–56. M.I. in Chancel,
with Arms of Beaumont quartering
Mann; on a shield of pretence Vesey
=Elizabeth, daughter and coheir of
Thomas Vesey of Sproughton [whose
sister Mary Vesey married John Vere
and John Beaumont of Sproughton
(ob. 1743)]. She was buried at Witnesham, aet. 77, in 1791

Priscilla B.
Bapt. 1712.
D. 1745.
[? 1744, M.I.
in Witnesham
Chancel]

Mary B.
Bapt. 1716
=Edward Venn, M.D.,
of Ipswich

Elizabeth B.
Bapt. 1723. Ob. 1730.
Buried at Witnesham

Amy (Amanda) B.
o.s.p. 1779

Elizabeth B.
(born 11 July 1745). Buried
20 Jan. 1745/6.
Witnesham Register

Elizabeth Beaumont
daughter and coheiress.
(Bapt. 1748. Ob. 1822)
=Philip Bowes Broke
(ob. 1801) of Nacton

Sir Philip Bowes Vere Broke
1st Bart., K.C.B. (Ob. 1841.)
Captain of the "Shannon".
Of Shrubland Park
=Sarah Louisa, daughter of
Sir W. F. Middleton of Shrubland Hall

Major General Sir Charles Broke Vere
K.C.B. (1779–1843).
M.P. for East Suffolk

Sir Philip Broke
(born 1804), 2nd Bart.
Commander R.N.

Note. Contemporary Annotations in the Witnesham Church Register very satisfactorily confirm some of our identifications, at the same time supplying corrections to dates inscribed on Monumental Slabs in the Chancel.

"1710. The Reverend Mr Michael Beaumont, Rector of Waltham in Lincolnshire, Uncle and Father-in-law to ye present Incumbent, dyed suddenly Oct. 11, and was buried Oct. 14."

"[1716.] Mr Jonathan Beaumont, uncle of Mr Robert Beaumont, Rector of this Parish, died suddenly at Barham Church in the time of Divine Service Dec. 23, 1716, and was buried in the Chancel of Witnesham December 26, 1716."

"1730. Elizabeth Dr of the Revd Mr Beaumont, Rectr of this Parish, and Priscilla, his wife, died at Ipswich, and was buried in ye Chancel directly before ye Altar Rails between the stones laid over Mr Daniel Meadows and Mr Hamby, Oct. 27."

"1745. Elizabeth Beaumont, daughter of Charles Beaumont, Rector and Elizabeth his wife (born July 11, 1745), was buried Jany 20 [1745/6]."

"Priscilla Beaumont of Ipswich, widow, first married to Richd Drury Esqr of Colne, Huntingdonshire, afterwards to Michael Beaumont, M.A., of Bildeston, Suffolk, died Jany 22d, and was buried Jany 26. Grandmother to C. B. now Rector."

"Priscilla Beaumont, Daughter of Robert Beaumont, late Rector of this Parish, and Priscilla, his wife, was buried Feby 6 [1745/6]."

If all clerical scribes had followed the example of the Witnesham Recorder, the writing of Parochial History would have been simplified. The dates cut on the plain slabs in the Chancel, with Coats of Arms completely worn away, have been in some cases inaccurately cut, possibly in the course of repair.

1 Peterhouse Admissions, p. 161.
2 Ibid. pp. 279, 280.
3 Ibid. p. 257.

www.ingramcontent.com/pod-product-compliance
Ingram Content Group UK Ltd.
Pitfield, Milton Keynes, MK11 3LW, UK
UKHW011913020325
455765UK00007B/43